TWO-TONED DRESS

Poems by
Lucy Adkins

BLUE LIGHT PRESS ◆ 1ST WORLD PUBLISHING

1ST WORLD
PUBLISHING

SAN FRANCISCO ◆ FAIRFIELD ◆ DELHI

Winner of the 2019 Blue Light Poetry Prize

Two-Toned Dress

Copyright ©2020, Lucy Adkins

BLUE LIGHT PRESS
www.bluelightpress.com
bluelightpress@aol.com

1ST WORLD PUBLISHING
PO Box 2211
Fairfield, IA 52556
www.1stworldpublishing.com

BOOK & COVER DESIGN
Melanie Gendron
melaniegendron999@gmail.com

AUTHOR PHOTO
Tom Adkins

FIRST EDITION

ISBN: 978-1-4218-3653-9

Acknowledgments

I would like to express my thanks to Marge Saiser, Amy Plettner, and the Cabin Girls on the Platte for their inspiration, encouragement, and thoughtful support, and in whose presence many of these poems first began to take form; to my teachers, mentors, and friends in the writing community who helped me keep on; and to Karl and Suzanne Kehm who provided a place to write. Special thanks also to the good people at Blue Light Press, especially Diane Frank for her generosity and wise advice, and Melanie Gendron for her beautiful work on design. Lastly, my eternal gratitude to my husband Tom for believing in me.

My thanks also go to the editors of the following journals and anthologies, in which several poems in this collection previously appeared, sometimes in slightly different forms: *Concho River Review:* "My Mother, Seventeen;" *The Cape Rock*: "Before the Vows" and "To the Other Side;" *The Briar Cliff Review:* "The Thing About Love;" *Poet Lore:* "White Cat;" *The Sow's Ear Poetry Review:* "The Drowning;" *Plainsongs*: "Grandma Ellen Tells it Like it Was." This poem also appeared in *Pudding Magazine* and the anthology, *Times of Sorrow/Times of Grace.*

Table of Contents

My Mother, Seventeen

— after Lyn Lifshin

I think of my mother, seventeen,
the night before she married,
her last night in her upstairs bedroom,
mid-August, hot. Outside, cicadas droned
against the tight bark of cottonwoods.
Heat lightning flared in the west.

At the foot of her bed stood the blanket chest
her father had made. And inside, gifts
from the church ladies' shower —
sets of dish towels, mixing bowls,
pillow cases, embroidered.

Marriage must have been a word
like mauve or corsage,
something exotic and fine,
something out of reach. But here
she was about to try it on

like the blue dress packed away
in her suitcase, the one she said
my father liked; and the white one
her mother bought for forty dollars,
ironed, and hung upon the door.

She must have wondered what it
would be like, her body like a blossom,
like a ripened plum, her body
a promise she had given,

and in the morning would wash
and dress, and her father,
as they say,
would give away.

Before the Vows

She made a list of what she would
and would not do. Cooking was fine,
jelly making, but no canning green beans,
no peaches in a jar. Occasional cobwebs
were acceptable. Dust bunnies.
But no spiders in the house, no roaches.
(That was before Alabama.)

And she would do her hair and makeup,
wear something nice when he came home.
She read a book about that once —
written by a man, a preacher, some family first guy
who told the story about visiting a parishioner,
a housewife, who coming on four in the afternoon,
told him he had to go. She needed to get ready
for her husband coming home. Pretty up.

He wrote how he admired that, how that
was the way it should be. He went on to write
some other things — about lingerie, and how
a woman should position her body, lean over when
dressing or undressing. She supposed
he thought you shouldn't hide under a bushel.
Not your peaches, anyway.

She wouldn't go that far. And she
would drive. Of course she would drive;
and work. But she thought the man's job came
first. That was the way things were, and there
was a line. She'd live close to that, and only
once in a while, step over.

To the Other Side

Like R. A. Dickey, the great knuckleball pitcher
in the making, the time he decided to swim
across the Missouri from Omaha to Iowa,
not knowing the treachery of the water,
how dirty it was, the undertows and whirlpools —
how he made it partway across, and realizing his danger,
turned back, struggling, half-drowning, his muscles
expanding and contracting, then losing power
like an engine wearing out;
and if not for his will, and the teammate waiting
on the shore — the shortstop,
reaching out to reel him in,
that would have been it.

In this way, our mothers and grandmothers
and their mothers before them
brought us into being,
starting out without Lamaze
and painkillers and epidurals,
starting out without husbands, sometimes,
struggling in breathless bedrooms
in hot waves of pain,
gripping bedclothes and bedposts;
and the hand of some other woman,
encouraging, exhorting,
willing them, willing us,
to come through, red-faced and gasping,
to the other side.

Writing Poetry

It's not like sorting socks
or making a cake,
or even (though that is pretty)
setting the laundry to flutter
in little flags out back.
It's more like taking your broom outside
to sweep the sidewalk.
You stop and pick up a piece of glass
and it turns into a memory from 1959.
It glitters at you, it shines,
and you don't think this will happen
but it slices into you and your blood is hot
and ready, and you are alive.
So you keep sweeping.
Mostly it's just leaves and twigs,
stuff that blows in from the street.
But once in a while, that glass.

Country Music

Disc after disc of Tammy Wynette,
Patsy Cline, Della Reece, Loretta,
and you develop a huskiness
in your throat as if you've spent

too many nights in smoky bars,
too many times your throat's
been swollen with tears. Maybe
you'll grow your hair long

and start looking for all the ways
your man has done you wrong.
Or thought about it anyway. Or sure
as sugar will do in the future.

Your posture will improve throwing
back your shoulders and bracing
yourself for all that life throws at you.
So you pull on your boots and find

yourself looking pretty good in the mirror,
and thinking about that guy next door
with long hair and tight jeans, how maybe
he isn't as hard on the eyes as you thought.

Selma, 1971

That summer, every afternoon
at two or two thirty, it rained,

clouds massed up, thunder
sounded in great cracks and booms,

and rain fell, hard and steady
for twenty or thirty minutes

of the world refreshing itself,
one drop at a time.

That was a time I was young
and newly married, jobless,

and in a strange land.
Strange to me, anyway.

I marveled at all that rain, how
dependable, as nothing else was,

a time every day you could
stop what you were doing —

the endless striving for,
or struggling against,

just go to the window
and watch magnificence

fall down out of a dark sky,
anointing the roof of the house,

the trees, the sidewalk
that led to my front door.

Vinegar

The tomatoes were red and plump,
the first of the season,

and I sliced them,
salted and peppered them,

sprinkled olive oil and vinegar,
snipped fresh basil.

Both from my garden —
the tomatoes and basil,

the vinegar like a sudden announcement
something like *we need to talk,*

or *hey you there,* something that
brings you up short, and you get

that twinge in your stomach.
That feeling you have

when the guy
you kinda like but shouldn't

leans in close. Anyway,
this is salad we're talking about,

and vinegar, one of those ingredients
you add that makes it all perfect.

The Thing About Love

It's a nice idea, my friend says,
but you can't varnish a piano with it.
And she's right. Though I've tried a time or two —
spreading it on thick with a bristle brush
or a cosmetic brush, or perhaps with a spatula,
flipping it over like a fried egg and letting it sizzle.
Maybe it's an off brand, you think. Or paint
and not varnish, not the real thing at all.
Yet you spread it on. And that piano,
it doesn't make music any more.

What you need is something you can depend on.
Like the earth in its orbit, darkness that comes
with each revolution, and then the light.
Maybe that's a kind of religion.
Still, I believe in love, and in pianos.
Music that comes to you from who knows where,
walking on a summer night. There are birds that walk
the ground, striding out like stalwart men
one foot after another; and birds on trees
that walk head first upside down. And live
their whole lives like that, perfectly content.

Breaking Off the Engagement

When she tried
to explain to her friends,
all she could say

was something about
politics, the books
he read, or didn't,

and the birds that
flew up in front of him
that he couldn't see;

and when he turned
the car one way, she
was thinking the other.

It was geography,
she said, continents
and drifting.

Thinking of Dorothy

— For Dorothy Wordsworth, 1771-1855

I imagine Wordsworth leaving
Dove Cottage on a June day,
rambling over the hills
from one great line to the next;
and think about Dorothy,
his sister, walking at his side,
every window of her heart
open for him, every door ajar.
Later, back home, I see her
making beds, scrubbing floors,
then rising to prepare his dinner —
a slice of beef, bread and jam, tea.
She places these offerings before him
while inside her, all the images
swirling, all the words with
their hack-saws,
trying to get out.

Typing Class

The goal was 70 to 80 words a minute
and she wanted to do that, sit
with her back straight, her fingers
poised just so; then it would be
a-s-d-f   j-k-l-sem   all morning long,
her fingers talk-talking with the keys,
the return chiming out one perfect line
after another. Quick brown foxes
jumped over legions of lazy dogs.
Early birds pulled up big juicy worms.
She rolled in sheet after sheet
of pure white paper, adjusted the bail
and typed on; and when she'd finished —
five minutes before anyone else —
she crossed her nylon-stockinged legs with a
satisfying swish, folded her hands in her lap
and let a big red-lipsticked smile
light up the whole room.

Old Photograph of My Mother

She is wearing a short sleeve
two-toned dress and is standing
on a bridge. It's a black and white
photo so I don't know the color of
her dress, though I imagine it in
two shades of blue. One hand
grasps her arm behind her back and
she seems tentative, beautiful as
she is — her slight figure, her dress,
the long dark curl of her hair.

She would be married in a month,
and maybe her shyness
is due to that; or maybe
it's because the bridge
she's standing on ends halfway
across the river. It's the Loup,
she told me once, that July of the flood,
when the rains wouldn't stop,
the soil turned liquid,
and it all ran into the river.

Her father is there in his suit
and hat, her mother, demure
in her Sunday dress. My mother
stands a little apart from them,
not far from where the planks
end, while beyond that is the river
at flood stage, swirling in eddies
of corn stalks and fence posts,
snags, and broken boards —
and below the waterline
all the splintered danger
she couldn't see.

Life With the Famous Painter

— Camille Doncieux Monet, 1847-1879

I put on my green dress
and he painted me,
sat with Bazille and Courbet
for the picnic in the wood.
That was nothing.
That was just time looking pretty
or pensive, staring off into the distance
to what was coming.

There was our home in Argenteuil
with the garden. I loved that;
and he painted me with roses all around,
sweet peas and cups of tea,
little Jean toddling about.
He could have married me sooner,
I'd have liked that;
and when sickness came
and Alice moved in to help,
he could have looked the other way.
He didn't mean me harm. He was just
a man, as people like to say
with a man's needs.

My life, he never knew.
The secret dreaming when he was off
in the fields with his easel,
or trudging away to paint the steam
rising from those dratted trains.
Always that light he was after
while I was after something
I couldn't quite name.
Maybe it was just someone to know me,

the way he seemed to know the dusk,
the sea, the shadows on the water —
the way they changed,
the way they stayed the same.

Swans

— *after a line by Lisel Mueller*

There are girls who should have been swans,
in some other world than this, some better world
than the way it has been for them. Like the three
young women in Ohio, stolen away at fourteen
years of age, seventeen, and twenty-one; and locked
in a shuttered house for ten years
in some crackle glass neighborhood,
some trash in the alley, graffiti haunted neighborhood,
and then broken out to the world.

I wish for them a quiet pond and time
to float in its water. I wish for them green
and red and pink and yellow, deep blue of a sky
too long denied; and I wish for them
the white rustle of feathers, beaks
to lash out at whatever evil chances by.

White Cat

He skulked at the edge of our campsite
watching us, a white cat, and I looked up
from where I sat by the fire to watch him back.
Look, I said, *maybe if he crosses our path*
that will mean good luck! And sure enough,
he padded on his little cat paws outside the edge
of the shadows and disappeared behind the car.
When he didn't appear on the other side
I got up and looked beneath, and there he was
positioned where the engine ticked and cooled,
where it still let off a little heat.

I saw then how his coat was matted and dirty,
how his sides caved in to his middle, his ribs
like the framework of a small boat heaved up
on some crag of shore. He hissed and his eyes
gleamed yellow, cold, and I knew he was
abandoned, lost, a small spark of fur and spit
escaped from a rock-heavy bag flung off the side
of a bridge. He hissed again and I backed off.

Later, I saw that he'd crept out and watched
us again from the shadows. I tossed a bit of bologna
from the cooler. He sniffed at it and flicked
his tail, but did not eat.

All day we had hiked and crunched through fallen leaves,
and there were bluebirds flitting in the bushes, innocent.
There were mice and voles beneath the crush of leaves,
living their lives, not knowing when the fox would pounce
or the hawk swoop down. Now it was late into fall.

That night, thunder and lightning.
The clouds let down a torrent of cold driving rain,
and the next day we awoke and packed in gray and cold.
From time to time, the white cat comes to mind,
and I like to think him grown larger and more fierce,
living in a leaf-choked culvert, not warm, but warm enough,
all the little birds around, in danger.

My Father, Reading

He loved Westerns —
Louis L'Amour, Luke Short,
but mostly Zane Grey,

every winter evening
in his brown chair
sitting with his book

and black coffee, riding along
with the hero in a land
of sagebrush and big sky —

one good man with his
buckskin and six-shooter
against all those desperadoes,

as my father was —
riding the tide of bad luck
and hard times,

and letters from the bank,
pink showing through
the windows of the envelopes.

In the Photograph

I am seven, I think,
and feeling pretty satisfied,
though my smile
is just a little one,

and in brown and sepia tones
you can't make out
the pattern of my dress,
but all these years later

I remember it tan and white,
a little black stripe, plaid
with ruffles down the front,
and a skirt that twirled and

danced around my knees.
But not now, not in this
picture, my lap full
of kittens, the mama cat's

third or fourth litter
that year, when everything
was bountiful, everything
in abundance:

rain at the right time,
the corn crop, all the lambs
and calves, and my mother's
and father's laughter at

the supper table, their
giddiness at times; and later when
I was in bed, their low murmurs
drifting up the stair.

The Drowning

It was later that the
bull rolled, and its carcass
swam from deep in the dam,
swam up stiff-legged, bloated,

swollen and uninsured.
I didn't see that.
I saw my sister ride her horse
like one of Pharoah's men

into the bloody Red Sea.
We knew about money,
the lack of it, the anger
of fathers. I stood out

of the way, safe, my heart
the thump of hooves on flesh,
saw futile thrash of limbs,
hot blood meet shock of cold

then the long glide under.
I saw my father's face,
the loss that could have been.
We have never spoken of this.

Grandma Ellen Tells it Like it Was

Back then
there was no Crisis Line,
no Friendship Home to take you in.
You had made your bed, and there you would lie.

So you acquired the proper downward glance,
learned just the right brush strokes
to keep the picture pretty;
and when his heel came down
you did what you must
and kneaded your rage
into a hard round ball.
It was poison,
but it was yours.
You kept it tight inside.

There is no disgrace
in sleeping with the enemy.
You did it for the children.
You did it to survive.

And more often than not
he would die
first.

The Times She Was Lonely

Once in the Sierra Madres
with the cloud floor low,
the mountains opened up
and there were valleys and valleys
of nothing but trees.

Many times at parties
with a drink in her hand,
smiling, cocking her head just so,
trying to glitter a little, to shine,
trying so hard,
but of course that doesn't work.

A time or two in the bathtub
with the water running,
crying where no one would hear;

and some late-summer afternoons,
air conditioners droning,
the sky dead,
cicadas sending out
their lamentations
from the trees.

What She Wants

She wants everyone at the table, all together,
though we are too many. But no adult table,
no kids' table. Stretch the frame out and put in
all the leaves, card tables at either end.
Pile Sears catalogs and telephone books
on the chairs for the three and four year olds,
pull the babies' high chairs close. Never mind
little hands patty-caking the mashed potatoes,
never mind splash of gravy, spilled juice.
Spread out the big white tablecloths,
three or four of them, and if
the cranberry sauce spills, it will come out.

She wants the daughters to cease their quarrels,
forget the old hurts, the real and the imagined;
and for the sons-in-law to behave themselves.
She wants it all perfect the way she sees perfect,
with food passed round and stupid jokes, and
afterwards, a mound of dirty plates and cups
and silverware piled high on the counter.

In the Flower Garden

It was May, one of those blue sky days
I'd been waiting for. I put on my old jeans,
my gardening shoes, gloves, took the plants
out to the garden — hostas, coreopsis,
black-eyed Susans. I arranged and rearranged —

got down on hands and knees, placing purple
alongside yellow, rounded leaves next to lacy ones.
Come on, I told my husband, *dig this hole here —
and here.* The soil crumbled in my hands and
I mixed compost, loam, patted the plants into place.

One hundred years ago, did my great-grandmothers
feel like this? Making, creating? Following a plan
of their own and waiting for the results? I like
to think so. Accepting gifts of iris from neighbors,
peonies, planting snowball bushes, bridal wreath spirea —

the names as lovely as the plants, speaking
them like chocolate cake in the mouth.
Of course they planted potatoes, cabbage, and
beans. They grew pumpkin, squash, corn, and
watermelon. Sent their kids to weed and hoe,

pluck off hornworms, potato bugs. Drop them
in cans of kerosene. But they had moonflower,
zinnia; they had bleeding heart and cosmos. Pinks
and blues and yellows. Their perfumes as night
came on, drifting through the air.

About the Author

Lucy Adkins grew up in rural Nebraska, received her undergraduate degree from Auburn University, and her MFA in Creative Writing in 2016 from the University of Nebraska at Omaha. Her poetry has been published in many journals, including *Rhino, Northeast, South Dakota Review, Concho River Review*, and the anthologies *Woven on the Wind, Times of Sorrow/Times of Grace, Crazy Woman Creek*, and the *Poets Against the War* anthology. Her chapbook, *One Life Shining: Addie Finch, Farmwife* was published by Pudding House Press. She has also co-authored a book of non-fiction, *Writing in Community*, which won an "Ippy" in the Independent Publisher's Book Awards.

www.ingramcontent.com/pod-product-compliance
Lightning Source LLC
Chambersburg PA
CBHW021917040426
42447CB00007B/909